Cultivating And Nurturing A Strong And
Fulfilling Marriage

Series 1

MARRIAGE PREPARATION
FOR
SINGLES

A Practical Handbook for Building,
Maintaining and Enriching a Lifelong
Christian Marriage

Jeremiah Rosaline

Table Of Contents

Jeremiah Rosaline

INTRODUCTION

An old saying goes, "Marry in haste and rue at rest." Getting married without proper preparation is equivalent to doing so, and the result will be regrets, extreme behavior, and, eventually, divorce. You should also be aware that the longer your relationship and engagement, the more stable and content your marriage will be. Conversely, the hastier your wedding, the sooner it will end.

It is an odd and regrettable circumstance that every day, several young men and women get married without doing any immediate preparation for the difficult work that lies ahead. No one would ever imagine getting a handyperson, a mastermind, a croaker, or counsel without any internship or medication.

The Pope argues that severe medication is required for one to be married and lead a happy marriage if people can plan for several

months and times to come mechanics, attorneys, croakers, nurses, and masterminds.

It is crucial for the couples themselves because marriage bonds require them to sanctify themselves and work out their deliverance, which isn't easy. It is essential for the sake of their children, who stand to gain or lose so much from the example of their parents and the home atmosphere. It is critical for the church because the health of the church depends in large part on the soundness of Christian sermons.

In the first section of this book, we want to talk about how to get ready for this new form of life or vocation called MARRIAGE.

Chapter One

MARRIAGE'S INTRODUCTORY STAGES

"A man shouldn't be by himself. I'll make him a good friend (Genesis 2:18).

According to the Bible, being alone is terrible for both men and women. Additionally, it is concluded that they need to find compatible partners. Every man and every woman who wishes to be married should search for a decent, well-known partner.

How does one find this appropriate companion in today's complicated and fractured society? Wine and music can make you happy, but a good marriage is better, according to the Bible (Sirach 40:20).

You need help finding a suitable companion in a day. A phenomenon is required to make one discovery in a single day. A happy marriage also involves other factors. It has to be set up. And for that, a sturdy base is needed. The initial phases of marriage are when this rough foundation is laid.

These phases will get the pair ready for a fulfilling and long-lasting relationship.

FIRST STAGE: DATING

Are you dating what? Should a God-child date? Let's first discuss what courting entails to determine whether or not a child of God should partake in it.

A date is defined as an engagement or appointment for a specific time in Webster's Dictionary. Dating is a brief period spent with someone for companionship, getting to know one another, and enjoying one's current situation, usually without any immediate plans to get married. Dating is best described as a man and woman engaging in social activity without making a marriage commitment to

enjoy each other's company. The primary goals of courting are to have pleasure and get to know individuals of the opposite sex.

Boys and girls start dating when they decide to condition one another, typically in their early adolescence socially. Dating develops from the friendship between two participants in opposite sex.

Dating Generally Falls Into One Of Two Categories

a) Courtship for social and recreational purposes

b) Exclusive courtship.

Casual courtship is social courtship. There is no emotional connection involved. It's just a prearranged get-together for conversation and entertainment between a young man and a woman. You go on dates with a member of the opposing sex to enjoy having things to do and places to go. There may also be an intellectual gain, but there is little to no intention of getting married.

Unique courting is an alternative form of courtship. Only a small amount of emotional investment is needed. Additionally, it is a planned social gathering of manly and womanly individuals for intellectual, social, and recreational pursuits with a view to courtship, engagement, and marriage.

When two young individuals engage in "Special Courting," they agree to only date one another.

It is evident from the definitions mentioned above and descriptions of courting that it is a healthy social activity. There is nothing morally wrong with it. A manly and a womanly engage in social trade that could or

might not result in marriage. As a result, a child of God is still free to date, but he should remember the biblical commandment "do everything for the glory of God" (1 Cor.10 vs. 31).

SECOND STAGE: COURTING

What is dating? Unique courting leads to courtship, the time between special courting and becoming legally engaged.

By way of explanation, courting is the relationship between a man and a woman in which one pursues the other's affection with the express intention of getting married. It is the regular and attentive visits between a young man and a young woman to foster understanding and keep marriage in mind.

Spending time together for fellowship and getting to know one another while courting serves as a stopgap for eventual marriage. It allows the parties involved to consider their preferences, compatibilities, and peace while gauging God's intention for the union.

Couples thoroughly examine each other's emotional, moral, spiritual, and social traits during courting to determine whether a pair will create a successful marriage match. This is when the compatibility of the two individualities is tested.

Honesty and openness of tone are required in courting. It's time to reveal previously hidden bones or life to the partner. Some heart issues must be disclosed, such as known gravidity, actual gestation by another man, a child with another woman or a mama marriage, a transmissible complaint chord, a severe internal breakdown, financial debt before the wedding, hereditary disorders, etc. Disclosure will foster trust and lay solid groundwork for a successful marriage.

During the courting phase, the partners discuss a lasting relationship and make conditional plans for marriage. Any arrangements they make are particular and private, not comprehensive or final. They don't pick a date, make public announcements, or prepare for marriage. They carry on discussing getting hitched and their promising future together.

THIRD PHASE: ENGAGEMENT

Marriage results from honest and genuine courting. A couple may now decide to become engaged after some courtship.

Explain engagement. Engagement could be defined as the mutual knowledge of a man and a woman's anticipated marriage. There may be a formal or informal engagement or wedding.

A verbal commitment made by both parties to test their love for one another, their compatibility for marriage, and their growing familiarity are known as an informal engagement. One or both parties may decide to become engaged on a casual basis just out of desire.

The parties negotiate and sign a formal engagement in front of a religious leader or two trustworthy witnesses. It establishes a severe obligation that can only be broken in dire situations.

A couple exchanges their vows to get married by sharing a symbol that connects their loyalty. While some people taste one other's blood to signify engagement, others use rings.

During the engagement, a couple intimately announces their engagement, wraps up inquiries into each other's families and personal histories, and decides on a date for both a civil marriage and a church wedding.

During this period, a few critical conversations and decisions must be made without a doubt must be made. To avoid future problems, the couple should discuss and decide on the following throughout their engagement.

1. The religious question must be settled, including regular church attendance, family prayer, participation in church-affiliated religious organizations, and the unborn religion of the children in a mixed marriage.

2. Methods of birth control and the number of kids raised. What is the ideal number of children to have? Which forms of birth control are advised?

3. The family's financial situation and the method utilized to estimate it. Should she have a job? In that case, before or after having kids? What sort of account do you have to manage? Which is preferable, individual

accounts or shared accounts? Who is the plutocrat in power?

4. Compatibility issues with prospective in-laws. While some in-laws have entered heaven, others are unduly jealous and anxious.

Prospective couples should carefully evaluate the following criteria since in-laws are essential.

Are both sets of in-laws in favor of the marriage?

Have the in-laws' families interacted before, and how well do they get along?

Are the prospective in-laws happily married?

Does the religion of the in-laws match yours?

However, even if the couple wants to live alone, they can still legally get married if the answers to these questions are affirmative.

PERIOD SPENT IN COURTING

A common question is how long a courtship or engagement ought to last. It is delicate to react in detail to such a question.

To ensure they are compatible enough to coexist in a loving and fulfilling relationship, the couple must get to know each other well enough to understand each other.

Experience and research show that an engagement should be at least six months or repeated more than once. It holds for dating as well.

Although courting or engagement should take little time, neither should it happen too rapidly. Avoid hasty weddings since they frequently need to be corrected. Colorful authors have exciting things to say on various topics, including the engagement or wooing phase duration.

Father Lord gave an illustration:

The couple should be together for a sufficient amount of time to get to know one another well, experience various amusing and intriguing circumstances, identify how many interests they have, and determine the strength of their love.

However, the time they spend together should be short enough to prevent them from growing apathetic or giving in to potentially dangerous temptations.

She cautions against excessively long expressions of affection, while most churches prohibit overly quick ones. No set rules can accurately predict how long a courtship will last. It should last long enough for kids to get to know one another very well regarding temperament and personality. This can usually be finished in a period of

Six months or more.

In conclusion, there should be a short time spent on the courtship or the engagement. Six months is the very least, and once is the maximum.

The Advantages Of Courtship, Dating, And Marriage

We've already mentioned that wooing, courting, and engagement are essential pre-marriage transitory phases. One or more of these must be completed before getting married. Let's now look at the benefits of going through each stage as one prepares for marriage.

Advantages Of Dating

There Are Certain Benefits To Dating…

1. Social Trading

Courtship can help you meet people and create friendships. Everyone who deals with you diplomatically will unavoidably leave some of themselves behind. You can gain knowledge from people by dating.

A jerk, a blowhard, or a gossip could teach forbearance-related assignments! When you date multiple people, you'll have a baseline for comparison. You won't be tempted to act like the ginger bottle cover who thinks it's the most delightful spot in the world just because he's been there once.

Dating satisfies your demand for enjoyment and entertainment on a social level. If someone merely works, their personality will become uninteresting.

2. Character Formation

The human personality can change in any way. When we interact with people, we can positively or negatively impact their identity development.

When you interact with a member of the opposing sex while dating, you'll discover more about yourself. The knowledge you get will help help you learn how to interact with people. You know something new about yourself and how your personality affects contraceptive sex with every person you date.

3. Maturity In Understanding The Opposite Sex

Relationships between men and women have different characteristics and tactics. Dating gives you access to various personalities, places, and contraceptive sex -related difficulties you might not otherwise have. As a result of similar exposure to the opposite sex, you'll begin to detect specific differences and discover how to relate to them.

4. Satisfaction Of The Enduring Need For Love

Every living creature has a natural yearning to love and be loved, regardless of age—whether they are a child, adolescent, adult, or senior. And the satisfaction of this requirement is necessary for average mortal growth and development. Dating helps to fulfill this fundamental human need for love.

5 Choosing A Life Partner For An Unborn Child

One of life's most difficult decisions is choosing a partner. It's challenging to find a partner you get along with. Marriage is not a learning process either. The connection is meant to be eternal. Dating helps you develop your critical thinking abilities so that, when you decide to get married, you can confidently assess the traits you want in a future spouse. Young people should date as many members of the opposing sex as possible to figure out what kind of spouse is popular and appropriate for them.

6. Spiritual Advancement And Development

It's not merely a social event when someone is courting. The drawback is that it denotes a crucial turning point and the beginning of a difficult journey leading to a sacred union in marriage. In a courting relationship, the partners experience spiritual growth. You see, dating is a precursor to marriage, and marriage is a perfect representation of the bond that ought to exist between man and God. Therefore, the relationship should stop if your dating life doesn't enable you to advance spiritually. Holy scripture states that the Lord is present "when three or more are united in the person of Christ" (Matthew 18:20).

Advantages of Courting

The benefits of courtship as an interim step before marriage include

1 .Social Security

Each couple was free to be themselves; unlike the first time they asked for or hoped for an assignment, they were not required to act in an attention-seeking manner. Also, providing emotional security is courtship. In their formative years, youths run into numerous skulls. They frequently get the impression that their parents, preceptors, guardians, sisters, and even the church are keeping an eye on them.

2. A Sense Of Value And Belonging

Courting shows trust, a magnet for commitment, and a degree of care that makes you feel special, increasing your love for tone-worth. Dating allows you to depend on someone if you have never had to, especially in the past.

Similarly, courtship boosts the confidence of the parties. You'll start reaching out to others and speaking up in groups because you feel more likable and valuable.

3. The Development Of Abilities For Human Relationships

As you get to know someone better, you become less selfish and more giving, which teaches you how to get along with individuals of different sex in bigger social circles? Courting has the advantage of teaching the pair about human relationships.

During courtship, the couple will also be able to pick up on specific, fairly general characteristics of the opposing sex and some of the preferences of the various relatives.

4. Cost-Saving Measures

The benefits of courting include cost-effectiveness and the ability to concentrate all your expenses on a single person.

They plan time together, such as watching TV at home or staying together and they keep track of their expenses. They can begin to enjoy their time together without incurring high costs because they are no longer trying to impress one another.

The Advantages Of Engagement

The congratulations and well wishes of the Musketeers will sound like music to the involved parties because no question is getting engaged fires bright passions in their lives. The couple also feels that they have suddenly attained a new status and finally arrived.

Engagement, There Are Some Significant Benefits.

1. Public statement

This public commitment made by the parties in the form of an engagement tends to strengthen the intentions of maintaining it because it serves as a public announcement to family and musketeers that a couple intends to wed and informs everyone that other interested campaigners have dropped out of the race and the future now belongs to the two engaged persons.

2. Honesty Tests

The pair has one more chance to assess their devotion to one another throughout the engagement time. A man might use an engagement to entice a woman into having a sexual relationship in a world where morals and values have declined. Relationships are casual and transient, while a woman might use the engagement ring to get a job or a visa for an overseas location even though she has no real intention of getting married.

3. Concluding Remarks

Before marriage, there is time for essential dialogues during the engagement phase. The pair has one last chance to evaluate their devotion to and affection for one another. Any unresolved arguments and problems that may have harmed their relationship should be brought up now.

4. Upcoming Programs

The pair can discuss their future and set partnership preparations throughout the engagement. It's a time for more in-depth discussions and reaching agreements on several specific matters, like when to start having children and how many, where to live after marriage and how to decorate the home, the style of wedding you'll have, who and how many to invite, etc.

Courting, Dating, And Engagement Disadvantages

Although courtship, wooing, and engagement provide advantages, there are also underlying concerns that should be considered.

1. Losing A Particular Identity

Some young people may experience identity issues due to dating and courtship. For instance, because her swain enjoys these things, Aggey enjoys football, salad dressing, and classical music. She has evolved into a carbon copy of her present honey preferences, like a weight. The importance of connection should be emphasized by courtship and courtship.

When she finally awakens, she'll probably feel worn out and frustrated since she hasn't allowed her personality to emerge.

The Bible cautions, "Don't let anyone lead your life for you as long as you have breath in your body" (Sirach 33 vs. 20).

2. The Effectiveness Of Repetition

Another significant concern is that dating and courtship frequently turn into routines. There is always a serious risk that a couple who has lost interest in one another may continue to be together. Maybe they've been so attentive and compassionate that they don't want to run into the danger of hurting each other too badly. As a result, the relationship went on unhappily and might have been marked by simmering animosity. Sadly, Sim, this might lead to marriage.

3) Extramarital Relationship

The desire to participate in sexual conditioning is a severe risk that courtship, wooing, and engagement expose young people to. A man and a woman could be inclined to have sex in bed after they begin to spend time together regularly.

It must be acknowledged that there will inevitably be intimacy when two individuals who spend a lot of time together engage in minimal physical contact and that sexual drive will typically develop due to increased communication and responsiveness. Consistent close connections frequently lead to adulterous sex in young individuals with high values.

Like a young man, a girl's body wants complete sexual expression. At first, females may not especially enjoy being caressed, but as things progress, a bit more kissing and cuddling become a natural evolution.

Couples courting or engaged run the risk of developing methods of reaching climax and alternative enjoyment without engaging in sexual activity. This could lead to developing a sexual pattern that could later interfere with the much deeper gratification of the perfect union in marriage.

Couples who indulge in these harmful practices risk creating a pattern of restriction or orgasm outside of intercourse that will be very challenging to overcome. They also risk affecting the atmosphere of sexual love in marriage.

4. An Early Or Illicit Union

When a woman engages in immoral courtship and courtship relationships, she runs the chance of becoming pregnant and suffers less social rejection when this happens; to avoid this, she may leave school or choose an impromptu marriage.

An additional immediate concern is a gestation or early marriage due to the possibility of adulterous sex.

Many guys would like to wed a lady who had at least as intense sexual experience as they did. In contrast, society doesn't often consider a woman with an extramarital pregnancy unfit for marriage.

It is ultimately the responsibility of women to cease adulterous sex since they are the ones who face social stigma.

5. Abortion

Revocation is a risk associated with courtship and courtship. Some ladies may discover they are pregnant while courting or courting, some may be enrolled in school, some may reside with their parents, and more significantly, some may experience denial from their sexual partners. Some young males may also claim their female prey isn't prepared for marriage.

To save their reputations, some young women who have been sexually assaulted turn to abortion; some do it with their parent's knowledge and consent, while others do so with the financial assistance of their male partners, and still, others do so covertly.

Everyone who voluntarily commits revocation is subject to a curse from God, and abortion results in cerebral pain and regret that hang on the victim for a very long time (Deut. 27 vs. 24).

6. Men Who Abuse Women

Sadly, some insensitive men today test, exploit, and dump young women unsuitable for marriage under the guise of romance and engagement.

It's awful that some young women feel they must get married to become famous before they die. Therefore, they offer their entire selves, body, and spirit to any man who vows to marry them. Sadly, these men waste the women's bodies by abusing them before returning to their town to marry fresh chasses, pure girls.

For men like them, the Bible delivers a message of guidance.

"Yow will propose to a girl, but another man will wed her" (Deut. 28 vs. 30)

7 Girls Who Victimize Men

Another unfavorable effect of courtship and engagement is the tyranny of men by their chosen women. Some men spend a lot of money to get their future partners trained in housekeeping, hairstyling, or fashion design. Others pay their rent, grocery, and clothes expenses while courting to change their minds at the last minute.

Some women argue that since marriage isn't necessary, they can change their minds, using phrases like "that man is too old for me" and "I can't marry that illiterate."

The Bible advises such women: "Do not fool yourselves; nobody mocks God. I wonder if these women remembered that these men were ineligible and too elderly to use their money when misusing them. You will reap what you have sown in life (Gal. 6 vs. 7).

NO-GO AREAS DURING DATING, COURTING, AND ENGAGEMENT

You are God's people, so you are forbidden to discuss sexual immorality, insensitivity, or capability among yourselves (Ephesians 5 vs. 3).

Can we kiss and clinch? It's up to a couple to decide how far they want to go beyond what is acceptable when they go on dates, appear in court, or become engaged.

One ought to be capable of evaluating one's behavior based on these. The Bible gives us guidelines for judging vessels with incorrect sex.

1. Giving And Receiving Kisses And Hugs Is Wrong.

Men shouldn't make physical contact with women (1 Corinthians 7 vs.1)

The Bible doesn't talk about handshakes or holding hands; instead, it talks about kissing and heavy hugs because behind the purportedly offending marking of kissing, hugging, and stroking comes to a sexually more arousing type of exertion. Kissing may or may not be the first point of sexual desire, but kissing often precedes subsequent pressure points, which start sexual intercourse.

Kissing and stroking are sinful behaviors by people who aren't reasonably married since they arouse the body's sexual desire.

Like a tree grows from its base, wicked behavior springs from passion. Unchaste behavior is like a poisonous snake whose head must be incontinently crushed to spit its poison.

2. Sharing A Bed Is Prohibited By Law.

It may be compared to a fire that burns everything it touches or a gravestone in a way that causes people to trip; sleeping in the same bed together gives a chance for sin. It's like a beer joint to a drinker.

Carrying an arsonist on fire into an area where hay, straw, and other combustible materials are kept is dangerous and wrong. It is also wicked to enjoy sinful activities, engage in sin, and carelessly expose oneself to a bad situation. The Bible cautions readers not to give the devil a chance to tempt them to commit sexual transgression (Eph 4:47).

Sirach 3:27 of the Bible states, "Whoever enjoys danger will become corrupt in it."

"Anyone who touches the navigator will become infected with it." Sirach 13 versus 1

The Bible cautions us that sharing a bed when courting, dating, or otherwise interacting is to love peril and to touch navigator, and that "whoever thinks he's standing establishment had better be wary that he doesn't fall" (1 Cor, 10 vs.12).

3. People Who Are Not Attached Are Not Allowed To Participate In Sexual Activities

According to Deuteronomy 22:20–21, "They are also to transport the girl outside to the front door of her father's house, where the men of her megacity are to beat her to death if the claim is valid there is no evidence that the girl was an abecedarian.

For some young males, the best way to demonstrate devotion to their ladyloves is by getting into bed. However, dating, wooing, or engagements are not the appropriate times to determine whether or not your prospective partner is capable of having sex, regardless of her wealth.

The Bible Warns That God Wants You To Be Holy
(1 Thess. 4 Vs.3).

Mary, Jesus' foster mother, asked, "How is it possible since I'm virgin?," in response to the archangel Gabriel's prediction that she would give birth to a son. Joseph and Mary had courted for extended times without defiling themselves." (Luke 1 vs.34) (Luke 1 vs.34).

2. Premarital Sex Frequently Results In Couples Breaking Up

People with opposing sex are drawn to one another naturally by the force of sex. If this sexual need is satiated outside marriage, the tendency is that the power that first drew the pair together will start to dissipate, and their interest in one another will wane.

Because once the "ultimate" has been obtained, there is little motivation to contemplate the mystery, couples who had sex before getting married tend to break up more frequently than those who did not.

3. Premarital Sex May Harm Mutual Sex.

Adulterous sex frequently occurs under less-than-ideal conditions, such as in a hurry, in the back seat of a car, at work, on a desk, or while standing in a shady spot. In these situations, along with the anxiety over being discovered and the possibility of becoming pregnant, the couple may have a wrong opinion of sex and misbehave. Additionally, the pressure to perform well may diminish the couple's pleasure. On rare occasions, it may even result in extreme anxiety.

4. Premarital Sex May Cause Rages Brought On By Guilt.

The likelihood that a woman may feel remorse and shame as a result of the encounter decreases as her level of devotion increases. When they break their moral rules, women feel guilt more intensely than men.

It's crucial to understand that comparable desires don't automatically disappear after marriage; for the majority of people, they will continue to linger. Adulterous sex was connected to those negative emotions before marriage to the extent that a person identified it with them. Examples include fear, guilt, and humiliation.

5. Premarital Sex 'S Impact On Sexually Transmitted Diseases (Stds)

Today, sexual contact can spread a variety of diseases, including syphilis, gonorrhea, genital herpes, genital knobs, cranks, AIDS (acquired vulnerable insufficiency pattern), and a plethora of others.

Numerous problems from STDs include palsy, heart disease, insanity, sterility, incapacitating injuries, huge ulcers, pelvic inflammatory disorders, uncomfortable genital abscesses, and cervical cancer, to name a few. Adulterous sex participants see themselves as high-profile STD advocates.

6. Adulterous Sex Can Develop From Premarital Relations.

A person who has had sexual experiences before marriage is likelier to behave recklessly after marriage. It's been said that habits are difficult to break. Before a wedding, sexual favors are challenging to snuff out.

7. Premarital Infidelity Harms One's Reputation

If a young woman gains a reputation for promiscuity, her prospects of finding a husband are minimal since no man wants to marry a hustler. Similarly, it will be tough for a young man to persuade his future bridegroom that he has real aspirations to marry and that he will be faithful to her after marriage if he gains a reputation for promiscuity. However, the BibleBible declares, "Put on thy clothing and cover her (Sirach 41 vs.12).

Jeremiah Rosaline

Chapter Two

How to Maintain Adulterous Chastity

Refrain from acting immorally. While sexual immorality is a sin against one's body, any other vice a man engages in has no bearing on his body (1 Corinthians 6 vs.18).

Every Christian has a moral duty to wait to start a committed relationship before giving up their virginity. In the sixth commandment of the Decalogue, God forbids this. Jews who lost their virginity were beaten as a form of retribution (Deut. 22vs.21). The Romans buried any abecedarian who disregarded her virginity alive. You may observe the severe penalties imposed on those who disobeyed chastity under Jewish and Roman law.

Chastity is very challenging to uphold. The Christian's best achievement, which takes the most work, is maintaining purity. The Church Fathers refer to it as martyrdom, even though it is a bloodless martyrdom that is in no way inferior. Death's short suffering makes it easy for the sufferer to join Elysium, whereas sustaining chastity requires a long, lifetime battle.

Now Let's Examine Some Innovative Ways To Maintain Adulterous Chastity.

1. Develop Worthwhile, Upbeat Pursuits

Your self-perception will influence how other people perceive you.

However, if you view yourself as cheap and sexually approachable, people will connect with you that way.

Others will believe the best in you if you live by your principles, and internal conflicts won't cause you to fall apart in front of others.

2. Talk With Your Partner About Morals.

To maintain your purity, you must set up some con-conduit rules. The Bible and your principles should be the foundation for these rules. You should exchange them with your pal. It would help if you created a strategy for easing difficult situations together. Limiting the amount of time you spend alone with each other and avoiding circumstances where kissing and caressing would be difficult to avoid are two ways to do this.

3. Avoid Situations That Are Intended To Pique Sexual Desire.

The Bible says to amputate your right hand and cast it on the ground if it causes you to stray. If your right eye causes you to wander, remove it and throw it away (Matt. 5vs.29-30).

The Bible warns us to avoid situations that could lead to mistakes. Know your location, the individuals you'll be with, the scheduled activities, and your anticipated return time before you're asked out. If you must visit your partner, attempt to limit how frequently you do so. If you see him too often, he can come to hate you (Prov. 25vs.17).

It is also advisable to travel with others rather than by yourself.

Aim to draw the draperies so everyone can see you and keep all windows open. Anyone who performs evil things despises the light because he doesn't want such actions to be made public, which is why (John 3vs.20).

4. Know The Facts Regarding Sex

"My people are destined because of their ignorance," says God's word (Hosea 4vs.6). Because they are unaware of sex, many young men and women struggle with sexual problems. The reality is that those who haven't had enough sexual education are more susceptible to sexual experimentation. Sexual curio could cause problems.

Along with ensuring you know the correct names and roles of the reproductive organs, you should take a sex education course and read a good book on the physiology of reduplication. Your trendy defense is knowledge. Your sexual life and schooling are intertwined (Prov. 4vs.13). Learning about sex is one of the best ways to maintain your virginity.

5. Exercise Self-Control When You Provoke Someone Sexually.

Tone management is one strategy for attaining perfection.

To control your sexual drive, you must be verbally restrained and engage in eye guardianship. Virginity loss is a severe issue for busybodies and irresponsible talkers. The soul is invaded by death through the window of the eyes (Jeremiah 9vs.21). The captain can allegedly be controlled by blindfolding him, and by tightly guarding our eyes, we may control our tendency toward evil.

Sublimation is another method for controlling your sexual inclinations. Your aspirations and requests will be sublimated into respectable settings. It implies that if you cannot satiate your sexual urges, you will look for another way to express yourself. A single woman can relieve sexual stress by writing, gardening, or playing tennis. A single man could select a career that will engulf all his interests and free time. He might develop an interest in organized religion, competitive sports, volunteer work, humanitarian groups, etc.

Sublimating sexual energy is identifying and developing interests and conditioning that provide you with enough unique satisfaction to divert your sexual stamina.

Sublimate your sexual inclinations as opposed to suppressing them. If you deny, stop, or pretend they don't exist, they'll soon reappear and put additional pressure on you. With the guidance of sublimation, you can accept and control your sexual desires more skillfully.

6. Engage In Religious Pursuits

Cast your worries on me since I'm keeping an eye out for you, as Peter said (1 Peter 5vs.7). One of the worries, fears, or trepidations that might be directed at Jesus or even your religion Include in your mastery your sexual phobias and worries. You must ask God for guidance in learning to control your urges. Sacraments, prayer, fasting, and meditation can all be used to accomplish this.

Fasting is a real help in keeping your virginity. The flesh is controlled by denying them food, just as how animals are ruled. "Be not drunk with wine, wherein is luxury," the supporter cautions (Ephesians 5:18). St. Ambrose claimed that eating and drinking cause the emergence of fleshly lust. Wine heats the blood and ignites the heartstrings of young men.

It is only possible to overcome one's tone with the means of grace offered by prayer and the sacraments. God's grace can only subdue the passion of nature; it is erroneous to think that one can control concupiscence and maintain chastity on one's own. No one is mainland until God permits (Wisdom 8vs.20).

Through forgiveness and concession, we are strengthened and equipped to fight sin.

By meditating on God's word, the desire for sexual fulfillment is removed. You won't have meat lusts if you walk in the Spirit (Gal. 5vs.16). Contemplation is a form of spiritual journeying. People who enjoy God don't look for other mannas; after tasting spiritual manna, earthly manna becomes boring, if not hated.

7. Make God's Presence A Resource.

No amount of concealment will keep a sinner from God (Job 34vs.22).

How was I going to escape you? Where can I go to get out of here? Verse 7 of Psalm 139

The one who remembers that God is everywhere and sees everything will not do anything that would displease Him.

Watch how Joseph responded to Potiphar's wife's attempt to hand him in.

"How could I behave dishonestly and break God's law? (Genesis 39 vs.9). Observe Susanna's behavior as well. She wailed, "I would rather be your innocent victim than rebel against the Lord" (Susanna 2vs.3).

Be conscious of God's presence wherever you are to keep from committing sins related to immortality. You'll be motivated to resist the urge.

8. Make Use Of The Flight Apparatus

It's fashionable to sin improperly by taking flight. Leave the immoral people and environment behind you. Because of this, light and darkness cannot coexist (2 Cor. 6vs.14).

Remember how Joseph responded to Potiphar's wife's attempts to pressure him into a sexual relationship with her? He got away. She coaxed him, grasping him by his mask, "Come to bed with me." He escaped, leaving her with his cover before running away (Genesis 39vs.12).

The most popular method of all the strategies to retain adulterous chastity is a quick departure from temptation. The apostle Paul counsels us to repress all straying urges. Still, he also urges us to abstain from sexual activity to avoid infection (1 Cor. 10 vs.6). Recreants win the Palm by restraining themselves from sensual entices and running away to safety.

9. Consider the Day of Atonement.

If the fire of pollution starts to burn within you, think of the eternal fire; the study will extinguish it.

"Remember your final moments in all that you do, and you'll never wander" (Sirach 7vs.36).

Mertinian, a hermit in Palestine, threw his bases into the fire when sexual cravings tortured him. If I couldn't manage the sweet honey, how could I endure the never-ending burning of hellfire? He wondered to himself as he screamed in anguish.

There is no doubt that young men and women's long-overdue chemistry has the same inclination to ignite the heart as burning straw does when it comes into contact with flames. Being cautious is a virtue in this regard.

How to Move on If You've Turned into a Disvirgined Young Person

But consider the period before you trusted Christ with your life.

If you've either willfully or unintentionally lost your purity.

In the past, God "ignored" your lack of knowledge of Him, but He now demands that everyone turn from their evil behavior (Acts 17vs.30).

The Sovereign Lord replies, "Do you think I adore watching a bad guy get killed? "No, I would rather see him repent and survive (Ezekiel 18vs.23).

The Lord said, therefore, let's settle this; come on. Even if sin has stained you scarlet, I will wash you until you are as white as snow. Despite heavy crimson stains, you will have white hair (Isaiah 1vs.18).

Before talking about what you should do if you have devirginized yourself, let's first talk about what you shouldn't do. To begin with, you must not feel unwell or animalistic. No one on earth consistently upholds morality and is faultless (Ecclesiastes 7vs.20)

Second, you shouldn't marry someone only because you had sex with them. Marriage is a choice made out of love, not lust.

Thirdly, you are not obliged to be married even though the gestation has resumed. Marriage is not a justifiable reason for a couple to avoid having a child referred to as a "bastard."

What should you do now that your purity has been tainted?

Here are a few suggestions.

Accept your mistake every hour; else, we'd be neurotic or unable to take responsibility for our mistakes. We claim it was an accident. The sooner you own your mistake, the sooner you can handle the problem and cope with the guilt that comes with it. Prophet Isaiah admitted to having unhealthy lips (Is. 65).

Jesus was admonished by the apostle Peter, who said, "Depart from me, for I am a vile man" (Luke 5 vs.8).

While they were at Jacob's well, the Samaritan woman told Jesus that she was unmarried (John 4vs.17). She was a liberated, spiritually open woman.

Once you are ready to recognize your sin, the next step is to make amends to your heavenly Father. Confession leads to inner healing. It repairs the damage caused by sin. It restores a strained connection to God. It mends your

wounds and absolves you of blame.
Additionally, it ends the nights of insomnia.

According to the Bible, God will uphold his
word and behave morally if we confess our
crimes. He will also forgive our transgressions
and purify us of all sin (1 John 1vs.9).

After talking with God, the next critical step is
to abandon sin and affirm your relationship
with your partner. It would help if you
decided to stop seeing each other as being
ahead. Maintaining your prior degree of touch
while promising to abstain from sex is useless.
It becomes impossible for a couple to remain
together without sex once it becomes a habit.
You must let your partner know that you've
decided not to engage in any more sexual
activities. You may speak to each other via
phone or writing, but you must forgo any
chance for privacy. Don't do the same sin
twice. Your initial training in the discipline
should be sufficient (Sirach 7vs.8).

Chapter Three

What To Look For When Selecting A Wife

When selecting a partner, two important considerations should be made:

(a) God's will

(b) A community that attests to God's purpose.

Marriage is a supernatural institution that is not regulated by the rules of this world. It was designed by the All-Powerful. As a result, it is crucial to seek God's face when making a marriage decision.

You may make your plans, but the Bible teaches that God will ultimately decide (Prov. 16vs.1).
Anyone who tries to hide their intentions from God will be destroyed.
The psalmist's advice to "ask the Lord to bless your plans" makes sense (Prov.16vs.3).
The careful consideration given while choosing a spouse is, without a doubt, crucial for the immediate treatment of a happy married life; one's choice of spouse can either substantially benefit or severely hinder the

other's pursuit of a Christian lifestyle. They won't have regrets about it forever, as well.

When choosing the person they will have to live with continuously in the future, those going to enter into connubiality should consider the pains of an indiscreet marriage.

They ought to accomplish this while keeping their attention on learning about God and the authentic teaching of Jesus. They should ardently pray for divine direction so that they might make their decision based on Christian wisdom rather than being driven by the blind, unbridled instinct of desire.

Unexpectedly, most young people already know who they want to marry. They often, consciously or unconsciously, fill in the blanks on their own as soon as they encounter someone who somewhat resembles that vision.

However, how can you tell if God is happy with the prospective spouse? While some enquirers rely on the stars, others consult compendiums and fortune tellers (divination).

Even if you and your potential mate are Tarsus, this proves that you were meant to be together. This is for followers of all religions!

The responses to several questions can ascertain God's support for the proposed union.

Is the man only seeking a partner for sexual activity?
However, God forbids that union because He wants you to be holy and devoid of all immoral behavior towards sexuality (1 Thessalonians 4vs.3).

Is the female too materialistic or worldly? If that were the case, the marriage would not be rescued since God detests materialism.
 Allegiance to the world is hostility to God (James 4vs.4).

The future couple must pray about their union to ascertain God's desire (Matt. 18vs. 19). However, the couples discover that their spirits aren't in sync and that, if feasible,

during prayer, they need to review or dissolve
their relationship.
God can connect two people by providing
them with spiritual harmony.

Think about Isaac and Rebecca's
circumstances. Abraham's slave randomly
chose Isaac's possible wife.
I'll ask a young woman to give me a drink of
water from her jar when she goes out to
collect water," he pleaded for assistance.

Please let her be the woman you have chosen
to be My son's wife if she accepts.
Rebecca is reported to have appeared and
fulfilled his wish before he could finish his
prayer (Genesis 24vs.43- 45)
Isaac noticed Rebecca and climbed down
from the camel.
They appeared to be in perfect harmony.

The Compatibility Phenomenon

Compatibility is one factor that should be
carefully considered while choosing a spouse.

Write about comity. It means "the capacity of two objects or individualities to unite in such a way that there would be little to no disunion in the union." Comity refers to a relationship between two parties that is harmonious and compatible. It indicates a collection of catcalls coming from related backgrounds.

Mate-Selection What to look out for A marriage will collapse if two people are incompatible as a platoon, so courtesy is vital when picking a partner. Given the problems that would arise from combining two creatures of different sizes and powers, it makes evident that the Mosaic Law outlawed such an act (Deut. 22vs. 10).

The compatibility of their age, religion, health, personality, and education must therefore be carefully considered by prospective couples.

i. Age

When picking a partner, age plays a significant role.

Because they are wealthy, some women marry men who are old enough to be their fathers. Some assert that they seek an older man who has given up on life, have found a wife or wives, and can be patient with them. Similar women are putting themselves in significant danger when dating because marriage involves much more than money and care.

To dominate and control them, some men also want to marry ladies who are more significant and younger than they are. For some reason, which they may shape to suit their preferences, they like girls. I want men who are comparable to realize that a relationship is not like a military barracks where you rule your troops.

There are certain disadvantages to marrying a famous person older than you.

Firstly, their union will result in sexual problems as they age if the man is substantially older than she is when they are married—say, let's say she is 30 times older and he is 45 times older. He is 60 and beginning to show his age, whereas she is 45 and still a young, energetic woman. The man cannot physically satisfy her sexually at this time due to their differing ages. Unless they are assisted by medicine, many men their age can fulfill the sexual needs of a 45-year-old woman.

In this situation, the man can become wary and untrusting, while the woman might be tempted to seek out greener sexual pastures elsewhere.

Secondly, there may be social problems due to significant age discrepancies in marriage. For instance, the woman could be hesitant to accompany the man to social gatherings since he might perceive her as his son rather than his wife.

Additionally, the woman can perceive the man as being out of touch with contemporary society, too traditional, or old-fashioned if he discusses social, artistic, and ethical issues with her. On the other hand, the male may consider the woman to be a filthy child who doesn't respect his culture. Since it is uncommon for both parties to share the same viewpoint on a subject, there will undoubtedly be differences of opinion.

Thirdly, there may be profitable issues. Even though most women now contribute to family support, men still make most of the household income.

Significant age disparities, however, usually lead to the woman shouldering most of the family's obligations since the male has either passed away before her, is retired and unemployed, or is physically unable to care for the family.

After all, the man ought to be older than the woman. Examples from the Bible include:

- The difference between Adam and Eve.
- The age difference between Abraham and Sarah.
- The age difference between Isaac and Rebecca.

Every marriage involving two people more than ten times apart in age should be properly thought out. A happy marriage generally accepts no more than a ten-fold age difference. In general, a man should avoid marrying a woman much older than he is.

Experience has shown that a significant gap naturally creates a barrier to the happiness and harmony of the marriage.

(ii) Religion

The importance of religion, which is suitable for marriage, in choosing a mate is also significant. As a result, it is suggested that you consider the following criteria while choosing your partner.
Which religion does the person you wish to marry practice?
Are they Christians, Muslims, or idolaters?
What does their faith entail?
Are their experiences with religion and their religious views congruent with yours?

Religious conflicts between husband and wife, or between parents and children, are a problem in many families today. In the absence of mistrust, religion considerably aids the marriage's success.

It's fascinating how different ideologies and philosophies have varied viewpoints on life.

Additionally, a person's religious convictions frequently influence their employment choice, manner of life, how they educate their children, and which musketeers they select. Therefore, it makes sense to wedding someone who is religiously compatible with you.

You are or have been one if you are a devoted adherent of any religion.

Your spiritual commitment, ideals, and stations were ingrained in you during your early nonage years.

These particular principles must be more deeply embedded to be noticed or quickly abandoned.

Most often, demands religious tolerance serve as a trap for the party making the request (you can attend your church; I'll attend mine).

Sadly, these assurances still need to be fulfilled. In other cases, the man wins the woman over to his faith or church, only to abruptly cease going to church once they get hitched.

Prospective couples should refrain from getting married to people of other faiths due to the risks involved.

Some questions might make you reevaluate your decision to wed someone who practices a different religion. Is either of you willing to practice the faith of the other?

If not, do you intend to attend church or visit each other's place of deification alternately?

Will one of you entirely compromise on their values or religion?

If you did this, how would you feel?

What would the musketeers, your parents, and your relatives think of it?

What will happen to your children if you both decide to keep practicing your current form of religious harmony?

Which religion will they be raised in?

Will they visit either one, both, or neither deification site? How do you handle the subject of family planning?

Contraception is supported by some religious organizations, while others oppose it.

The significance of religion to a husband and wife's happy and fulfilling union cannot be emphasized. As a result, it's crucial to consider religion carefully when making marriage decisions.

iii. Personality

It's essential to carefully consider the personality features of the person you wish to marry and spend most of your life with.
A disposition is one of the most important characteristics when selecting a companion.
It's unlikely that someone who lacks tone control, enjoys barrancas, cannot express good desires of affection and love and excessively suspicious, lacks respect for others, cannot tolerate minor erraticism from others, is overly emotional, and is aggressive will make a good husband or wife.
A surplus of these traits will be detrimental to a solid interpersonal bond. These should all be acquired during the courting or engagement. Being quick to anger is a hallmark of infancy and seriously destroys harmonious marriages.

Control of one's temper is a characteristic that needs to be examined and exercised to develop a mutually beneficial relationship. One of the leading causes of marital conflict is being too opinionated or narrow-minded.

It takes giving in and being open to your spouse's point of view to have a happy marriage.

Narrow-mindedness is a reflection of dogmatism and intolerance. It tends to act quickly and to be skeptical and critical. Emotional maturity is a significant personality trait. It is essential for a fulfilling marriage. Being emotionally mature involves:

- Having a relaxed tone.
- Being friendly and professional.
- Accepting responsibility.
- Being independent in thought and deed.
- Being tolerant and patient, flexible and adaptable.
- Expressing anger in a way that is acceptable to others.
- Loving someone other than oneself.
- Accepting others for who they are.

One should look for a potential partner who shares a high level of maturity, even though perfect maturity is uncommon.

iv. Health

Genuine health comity between partners is necessary for a satisfying and long-lasting covenant. According to an African saying, since all lizards lie flat on their bellies, it can be challenging to determine whether someone is feeling stomach pain.
According to an old English saying, not everything that glitters is gold. The Bible also cautions against passing judgment on someone based on their appearance or comments (Isaiah 11vs.3).

The extent to which our clothing conceals us from the wider population makes it challenging to constantly know who is healthy or ill. Conducting a deceptive investigation on the medical history of the family, you wish to affix yourself to, is essential. Some conditions or personality traits are inherited and run across many families.

Internal illnesses, epilepsy, sickle cell anemia, leprosy, low IQ, and countless other disorders are among them.

It would help if you scanned your potential partner's present health for hereditary disorders piecemeal.

What, for example, is your genotype?

Are you an SS, AA, or AS?

How about your prospective love interest?

Are you compatible physically?

Regardless of how much you love each other or how long you've been together, you should pay close attention to your unborn partner's health. If you need more clarification about someone's health, don't rush into marriage with them.

When choosing a spouse, one should consider the person's educational level. Are you appropriate for each of our specific educational needs? Your marriage may have issues if you are "nearly uneducated" and your prospective spouse is "too educated."

The educational backgrounds of the pair are so radically dissimilar that many marriages nowadays are on the verge of dissolving. It is improper for a graduate to marry a former student of a primary academy.

They don't collaborate academically. This does not, however, suggest that if they get married, their marriage will end badly. They can have a successful relationship if they are emotionally responsible and have a shared understanding.

Jeremiah Rosaline

76

Chapter Four

The Selection Of A Partner By Parents

This chapter is divided into two parts: the function of parents in mate choice and the necessity of premarital counseling.

The Function Of Parents In Selecting A Spouse

The fact that parents have such a big say in who their kids will marry is revolting. Any young person should talk to their mothers if they get sincere about someone. Parents must remember that they lack the power to force a way of life on their kids.

A person's decision to get married, remain single, or adhere to a particular faith is their own. Parents must coach and advise their children, but they need additional power. The same guidelines apply when choosing a life partner.

Why Parents Should Be Involved In The Selection Of Partners

Numerous justifications are possible.

FIRST and foremost, the man and woman should take their parents' wise advice seriously and not disregard it while choosing a companion. They can avoid making a mistake by doing this because they have a mature understanding of and experience with dealing with mortal affairs. When they are about to get married, they can better accept the heavenly blessing of the fourth degree. Respect your parents to ensure a good outcome for you and a long life in this world.

SECOND, parents desire to attend their children's weddings.

Nobody cares more about the person you'll eventually marry than your parents. When you get married, they feel delighted and honored. They think their parental obligation has been fulfilled by witnessing them wed to a compatible companion.

The Bible says of parents: "Giving your son in marriage signifies the accomplishment of a great duty, but sees that she is given to a prudent man" (Sirach 7vs.25). But how can they introduce you to an intelligent man or a good woman if you don't ask them?

THIRD factor is how much parents spend on their children.
Because they have spent a lot of time and money raising you, you must consult your parents for advice before selecting your partner. You didn't give your life; they did. They raised you from infancy, took good care of you, and kept you close to them.

They have sacrificed some of their most stylish moments to meet your requirements. They selflessly offered their cash and time to provide you with food, clothing, sanctum, and various amusing treats.

Why don't you consult them when you're ready to tie the knot? Why shouldn't you consider their perspectives while choosing a life partner? Never forget the suffering your mother endured while carrying you, and honor your father with all of your heart (Sirach 7vs.27).

FOURTH, they experience a vision. Another reason to ask your mother's counsel is that she can see future effects that you cannot. Some of the issues you're presently facing have already been resolved by them. They can also foresee future troubles you might have because of their visitors. Most likely, out of special love and concern for you, they will draw your attention to specific problems they want you to be aware of.

FIFTH, they can adopt a more sensible attitude. Because they were not personally involved in the matchmaking, your parents might be more reasonable. They can learn more about the general state of affairs. You consider it to be a matter of being in love. However, your parents understand that marriage demands love and duty. They might highlight fundamental problems that make it difficult for you to have a happy marriage. They could advise you to take your time and calmly and logically weigh the possible outcomes.

"Slate hair, good discernment, and sound advice create a great combination," the Bible says. Older people "wear the experience crown" (Sirach 25vs.4.6).

SIXTHLY, parents don't mistreat their children. It's ridiculous that your parents would choose to encourage you to achieve lasting happiness instead of restricting or obstructing it. They want to share knowledge and tasks with you that they may have had to learn the hard way. They aim to shield you from future issues if you choose poorly today. That your parents want to determine whether or not you should get married makes it reasonable. The thought of having grandkids excites them.

Making your parents proud of you will make your mother happy, so remember that (Proverbs 23vs.25).
The family name holds a lot of significance for parents. Parents advise their children on who to marry and pray for their actions and decisions to reflect well on their family.

Why is this important? It implies that your parents expect that by the time you move out on your own, you will have acquired enough morals and values to honor them, your family, your community, your church, and society. They are hoping that you will choose a partner they can get along with and fit in with the family.

Friend, please believe that your parents significantly influence your decision to marry. They must be talked to, and the problem must be discussed with them. Based on their past experiences, they are confident that their life mate will be crucial to their future happiness. Consider things from their standpoint for a while.

A Need For A Sturdy Wedding: Premarital Counseling

Many young people get married too soon and without any planning. Some people are forced into marriage by their families or musketeers.

Some people marry their age-matched partners. Union calls for a certain level of maturity, including the use of both your mind and your heart, which needs to be understood by these young men and women.

What provides adulterous comfort? It is a particular type of technical comfort designed for engaged couples.

It involves a series of meetings, conversations, and consultations between the couple and a knowledgeable counselor—typically a skilled married counselor or a religious leader.

The following topics will be covered in the counseling sessions:

i. The motivation behind the engagement

ii. How are things in your current relationship?

iii. Previous marriages

iv. A discussion of personal backgrounds, beliefs, and education

v. An examination of the several needs each spouse in a marriage might have, including love, acceptance, appreciation, communication, sex, and financial demands.

vi. Talks of starting a family, acquiring a job, etc.

Adulterous soothing aims to guide the couple in dealing with people and circumstances that could affect their marriage. Thanks to it, they are learning how to have a successful marriage and race.

Adulterous soothing exposes the husband to factors that might or might not be a factor in marital problems.
These include the couple, other people, and associated circumstances.

1. Each Member of the Couple

The pair could be the cause of their problems in several different ways. There are indeed substantial character variances. No two people are the same, despite how similar they may seem.

A problematic one of their undesirable habits could arise. It could be excessive drinking, cheating, sleeping in, excessive demand for sex, inability to hold down a job, egoism, etc., on the man's end.

On the woman's end, this could manifest as flirting, failing to keep the house clean, forgetting to make dinner, spending too much money on jewelry or cosmetics, not being able to satisfy her spouse sexually, neglecting the family, and so forth.

2. Other Person(s)

Marriage issues might arise from people other than the partners themselves, such as kids, in-laws, neighbors, Musketeers, coworkers, cousins, apprentices, or housekeepers.

3. Other Issues

The family extremity may also result from other factors, including postponing childbearing, a lack of children, the children's gender—male or womanly—the absence of manly challenges, poverty, poor health, a partner switching to a different religion, an adulterous relationship, and others.

By having a firm understanding of what a married partnership involves and how to maintain it, the couple will experience total and thorough adulterous healing. As a result, they will be able to transition into marriage more swiftly and efficiently. Their chances of having contented offspring will increase.

Last Chapter

The Conclusion

In the final chapter of "Marriage Preparation for Singles," we stand at the threshold of a new beginning, armed with wisdom and a profound understanding of the sacred covenant that is marriage. As we conclude this transformative journey, let us reflect on the words of the Bible to infuse our understanding with timeless wisdom.

The Bible tells us to "Trust in the Lord with all your heart, and do not lean on your own understanding; in all your ways submit to Him, and He will make your paths straight." The importance of direction and faith as we begin the journey towards marriage is emphasised in this poetry. It emphasises the need of having faith in a higher power and relying on divine guidance in our relationship.

Paul the Apostle words in 1 Cor. 13vs.4:7 beautifully encapsulate the essence of love, stating, "Love is patient, love is kind. It isn't egocentric, it's not jealous, and it's not haughty. It is not self-seeking, does not defame others, is not quickly enraged, and does not keep track of wrongdoings. Love rejoices with the truth rather than taking pleasure in wickedness. It always defends, always believes, always aspires, and always endures. The virtues we ought to strive for in our marriage are illustrated in these verses, which emphasise the importance of love, tolerance, and forgiveness.

As we conclude our journey through "Marriage Preparation for Singles," let us remember Eph. 5vs.25, which instructs, "Husbands, love your wives, just as Christ loved the church and gave Himself up for her." This verse is a profound reminder of the selflessness, sacrifice, and unwavering commitment that should be at the core of every marriage, echoing the message of mutual love and support.

In closing, this book has served as a compass, steering us toward a deeper, more meaningful understanding of marriage and the divine principles that guide it. With the grace of God and the wisdom of His word, we now step forward into the world of relationships and marriage, equipped not only with practical knowledge but also with a spiritual foundation that will help us build a union based on love, faith, and enduring happiness. May our journeys be blessed, and your union be a testament to the divine love that binds us.

See You In The Next Series!